Hello, Family Members,

Learning to read is one of the most important accomplishments of early childhood. **Hello Reader!** books are designed to help children become skilled readers who like to read. Beginning readers learn to read by remembering frequently used words like "the," "is," and "and"; by using phonics skills to decode new words; and by interpreting picture and text clues. These books provide both the stories children enjoy and the structure they need to read fluently and independently. Here are suggestions for helping your child *before*, *during*, and *after* reading:

Before
- Look at the cover and pictures and have your child predict what the story is about.
- Read the story to your child.
- Encourage your child to chime in with familiar words and phrases.
- Echo read with your child by reading a line first and having your child read it after you do.

During
- Have your child think about a word he or she does not recognize right away. Provide hints such as "Let's see if we know the sounds" and "Have we read other words like this one?"
- Encourage your child to use phonics skills to sound out new words.
- Provide the word for your child when more assistance is needed so that he or she does not struggle and the experience of reading with you is a positive one.
- Encourage your child to have fun by reading with a lot of expression . . . like an actor!

After
- Have your child keep lists of interesting and favorite words.
- Encourage your child to read the books over and over again. Have him or her read to brothers, sisters, grandparents, and even teddy bears. Repeated readings develop confidence in young readers.
- Talk about the stories. Ask and answer questions. Share ideas about the funniest and most interesting characters and events in the stories.

I do hope that you and your child enjc

—Francie Alexander
Reading Specialist,
Scholastic's Learning V

D1402035

To Emily Sue, Chloe Jane, and Lily Mae
—J.O.

To my favorite bug lover, Doug
—J.Z.

Text copyright © 2000 by Joanne Oppenheim.
Illustrations copyright © 2000 by Jerry Zimmerman.
All rights reserved. Published by Scholastic Inc.
SCHOLASTIC, HELLO READER, CARTWHEEL BOOKS and associated logos are trademarks and/or registered trademarks of Scholastic Inc.

Library of Congress Cataloging-in-Publication Data
Oppenheim, Joanne.
    Big bug fun: a book of facts and riddles / by Joanne Oppenheim ; illustrated by Jerry Zimmerman.
       p.   cm.—(Hello reader! Science — Level 3)
    Summary: Information about the physical characteristics and behavior of different kinds of insects is accompanied by riddles featuring bugs.
    ISBN 0-439-08749-X (pbk.)
    1. Insects Miscellanea Juvenile literature. 2. Riddles, Juvenile. [1. Insects Miscellanea.
    2. Riddles.] I. Zimmerman, Jerry, ill. II. Title. III. Series.
QL467.2.066   2000
595.7—dc21
                                                      99-39190
                                                    CIP

10 9 8 7 6 5 4 3 2 1   00 01 02 03 04
Printed in the U.S.A.   24
First printing, March 2000

BIG BUG FUN

A Book of Facts and Riddles

by Joanne Oppenheim
Illustrated by Jerry Zimmerman

Hello Reader! Science — Level 3

SCHOLASTIC INC. Cartwheel B·O·O·K·S®

New York Toronto London Auckland Sydney
Mexico City New Delhi Hong Kong

There are more bugs in the world than any other kind of animal. Scientists have found more than 750,000 different kinds of bugs.

All Bugs Are Not Insects

Insects have six legs. They come in many sizes, colors, and shapes. Adult insects have three main body parts:

a head,

a thorax,

and an abdomen.

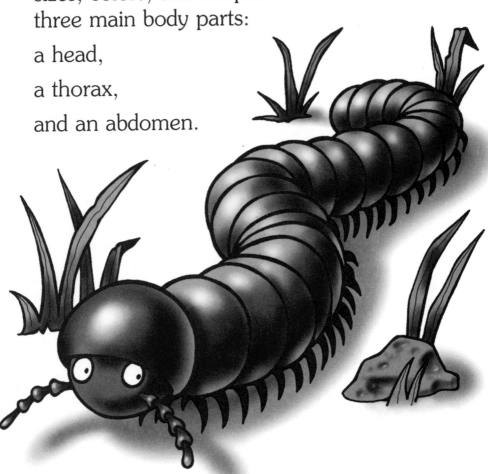

A **Centipede** is a bug but it is not an insect. Its name means 100 legs, but some centipedes have only 30 legs. Others have 300 legs! This bug can grow as long as 10 inches.

Of these three bugs, can you tell which one is not an insect?

ant

bee

spider

If you said the **Spider**, you're right! The spider is not an insect because it has eight legs.

Q. Which bug would you put in a piggy bank?

Giants of the Bug World

Goliath Beetles are the heaviest insects. Many are more than four inches long and weigh almost as much as a stick of butter—three and a half ounces.

Walkingsticks are the longest insects in the world. The body of a walkingstick can be over 12 inches long.

A. The cent-i-pede!

An **Atlas Moth** has bigger wings than any other bug in the world. From wing to wing, it can be 12 inches wide.

STRANGE BUT TRUE . . .

360 million years ago, in the days of the dinosaurs, there were giant **Dragonflies**. When they spread their wings, they were more than two feet wide!

The **Goliath Spider**, found in the rain forest of South America, is the world's biggest spider. It can have a leg span of 11 inches. That's as big as a dinner plate!

Q. Which bug should you take trick-or-treating?

Bugs of the Night

A **Stick Caterpillar** hardly moves all day. It sits on a branch, looking just like a twig. At night, it goes walking and feasts on leaves.

STRANGE BUT TRUE . . .

Spiders spin their webs at night.

Most moths sleep by day and fly by night. The **Black Witch Moth** scares bats and owls away with glow-in-the-dark spots that look like giant eyes.

A. The black witch moth!

This hairy **Tarantula** hides all day. At night it hunts for bugs, birds, and even snakes to eat.

Fireflies wink and blink to each other in the dark. They use their special lights to attract a mate.

Q. Which bug is the most religious?

Time for a Snack!

Cockroaches can eat almost anything. They will eat paper, plastic, and even leather. Maybe that's why they have lived more than 300 million years, since the days of dinosaurs!

Most bugs eat plants. A band of **Gypsy Moths** can eat all the leaves off a forest of trees. A swarm of locusts can destroy fields of crops.

A. The praying mantis!

But not all bugs can chew. **Butterflies** and moths sip nectar from flowers. They use their tube-shaped tongues like drinking straws.

Mosquitoes eat by biting people and animals for a drink of blood.

The legs of a **Praying Mantis** have spines to grab the bugs it eats. A female praying mantis may even eat her mate!

Q. Which bug might live in a castle?

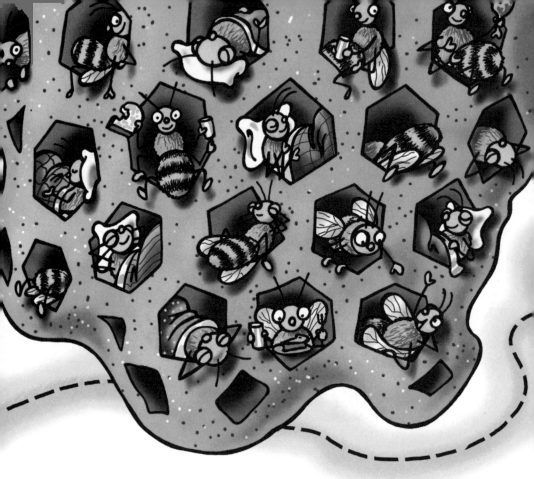

Brrrrrr...It's Cold Outside!

Most bugs stop flying, creeping, hopping, or eating all winter long.

Honeybees live through the cold winter inside their hives. They take turns eating and resting.

Some bugs spend the winter as eggs. The **Praying Mantis** lays hundreds of eggs in a papery case that will hatch in the spring.

A. The monarch butterfly!

STRANGE BUT TRUE. . .

Monarch Butterflies fly south every winter. They fly as far as 2,500 miles. That's a long, long way to fly! Millions of monarchs gather in Mexico and California where they stay warm for the winter.

Many bugs, like the **Luna Moth**, spend the winter inside cocoons. When spring arrives, the cocoons open—and bugs are on the move again!

Q. What bug should you take on a camping trip?

Abra-ca-dabra!
How Bugs Change

Tent Caterpillars camp out all day in a big, silky nest. At night they go out and eat leaves until they are fully grown. Then they go off to spin their own cocoons. In a few weeks, they will emerge as adult moths.

Most young insects do not look like the adult insects they will become.

A. The tent caterpillar!

Changing from egg . . .

to caterpillar . . .

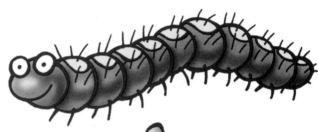

to pupa (in cocoon) . . .

to an adult . . .

is called a complete metamorphosis
(met-a-MORF-o-sis).

Q. What kind of bug might a
knight fight?

How Some Bugs Hatch

Dragonflies hatch underwater and have no wings. As they grow longer and longer, they outgrow their old skin. Pop! The skin splits. This is called molting. Each dragonfly may outgrow its skin 10, 12, even 14 times!

When it is fully grown, the dragonfly climbs out of the water.

Now it splits its skin for the last time. Soon the adult dragonfly with beautiful wings is ready to fly!

A. A dragon-fly!

STRANGE BUT TRUE...

Dragonflies may live underwater for one to four years! Once they leave the water, they live just a few short weeks. They mate, lay their eggs, and die.

Some insects like the dragonfly grow through just three stages. The young insect looks much like the adult bug it will become.

It changes

    from egg . . .

        to nymph . . .

            to adult.

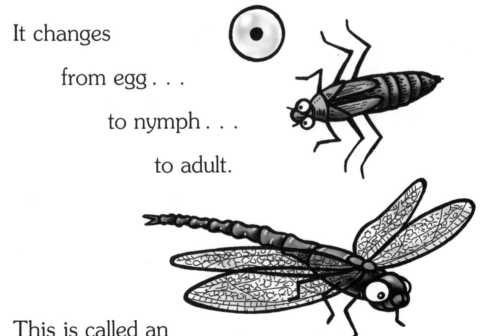

This is called an incomplete metamorphosis.

Q. What are the sweetest bugs in the world?

Getting Around

A **Grasshopper** can jump about 30 inches in one hop. If you could jump like a grasshopper, you would jump more than 100 feet in one giant leap!

STRANGE BUT TRUE...

Insects walk on three legs at a time—they use the middle leg on one side and the front and hind legs on the other. That's how they stay steady on their feet!

A. Honey-bees!

A **Housefly** can walk upside down on the ceiling because it has sticky pads on its feet that will stick almost anywhere. The housefly can also taste with its feet!

Honeybees have hairy "brushes" and "baskets" on their legs to collect pollen from flowers.

Water Striders can skate over the top of the water as they hunt for insects to eat. Waxy hairs on their feet keep them from sinking into the water.

Q. What bug is most like a kangaroo?

Buzz! Click! Trill!
A Buggy Symphony

A tiny **Mosquito** beats its wings 600 times in a second. That is the buzz you hear. It's the hum of its wings beating. Other bugs hear the sounds, too.

Grasshoppers not only hop with their legs, they sing with them! They rub the file (the rough edge) on their back legs against their wings, and this makes their trilling song.

A. A grass-hopper!

Katydids are nighttime singers that sing their own name. Rubbing the files on their wings together, they sing, "Katy-did, Katy-didn't."

STRANGE BUT TRUE...

Bugs don't have ears like we do. But they can hear vibrations in the air. They "hear" through tiny hairs on their bodies or with their antennae. **Crickets** even hear through their knees!

Cicadas don't rub their wings or legs together to sing. Their buzzing song is made by organs in their abdomen that vibrate like drums.

Q. What bug sounds like a clock?

Buggy Pests

Bedbugs are blood-sucking parasites that come out at night. They do not live on people or animals, but in their beds and nests.

Head Lice or **Nits** feed on blood from people's heads. They glue their eggs on people's hair.

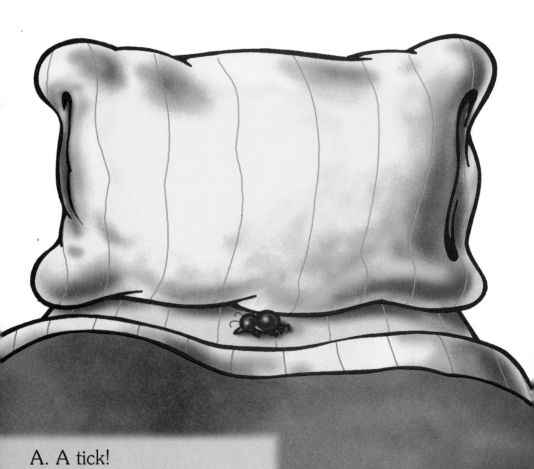

A. A tick!

Ticks attach themselves to animals with their strong mouths. They suck blood for days and days. Some deer ticks carry bad diseases to people, such as Lyme disease.

Fleas are tiny, tiny parasites that live by sucking blood from birds, animals, and people. They jump on and off the animals they are biting.

A tiny flea can jump more than a foot in the air. That's 200 times the size of the flea itself!

Q. Which bug tastes good with toast?

Is It a Moth or a Butterfly?

Can you tell a **Butterfly** from a **Moth**? Both butterflies and moths have wings that are covered with scales. They both have tube-shaped tongues for sucking up nectar. They roll their tongues up between drinks.

A butterfly resting holds its wings up and together.

A moth resting holds its wings out like an airplane.

A butterfly's antennae are thin like a thread with a knob on the end.

A moth's antennae can be thin or have a feathery shape.

A. A butter-fly!

A butterfly's body is long and thin and has no hair.

A moth's body is thicker and hairy.

Most butterflies fly by day.

Most moths fly by night.

Most butterflies are brightly colored . . . but some are not.

Most moths are not brightly colored . . . but some are.

Q. What's the hottest bug?

Beetles, Beetles . . .

There are more beetles in the world than any other kind of bug. You can find them in all sizes and colors. Beetles live almost everywhere. Pick up a stone and you will probably see a beetle run away.

Some live their lives underground. Others live in the water. **Whirligig Beetles** have eyes that can see above and below the water.

Most beetles have two pairs of wings. Their hard front wings work like armor to cover and protect the soft back wings they use for flying. Beetles have strong mouths for chewing, and they eat everything from bugs to bark.

A. A fire-fly!

Stag Beetles have giant jaws for fighting each other. Male stag beetles fight over female stag beetles. The beetle with the biggest, strongest jaws is the one who wins.

STRANGE BUT TRUE . . .

Fireflies are beetles, not flies!

Tiger Beetles shine like metal of purple, green, or blue. Running or flying, these bug-eaters move faster than most other beetles.

Q. What bugs have the best manners?

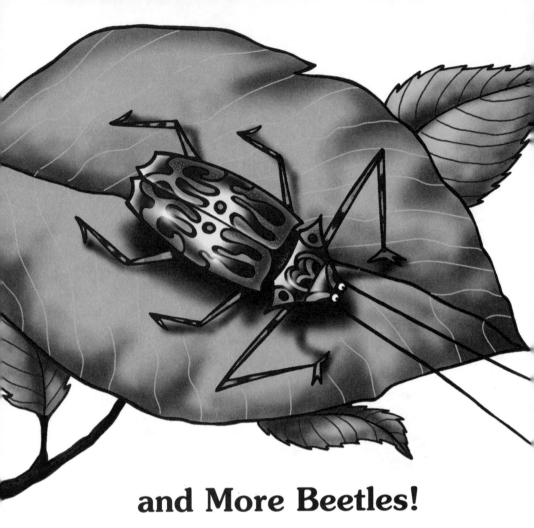

and More Beetles!

The **Giant Longhorn Beetle** lives in the treetops of the rain forest and eats leaves at night. Its super-long antennae can be three times longer than its body.

If a **Click Beetle** lands on its back it can bend its body, spin, and flip. This makes the "CLICK" sound that gives the beetle its name.

A. Lady-bugs!

STRANGE BUT TRUE...

Not all ladybugs are red and black. Some are white, yellow, pink, and even orange. Baby ladybugs have no spots for the first 12 hours. When they are grown, they can have as many as 13 spots.

Ladybugs are beetles. Farmers often use ladybugs instead of insect spray. Ladybugs eat bugs that would eat farmers' crops.

Q. What bug is like glue?

Now You See Them, Now You Don't!

Many bugs stay safe because they are hard to see.

It's hard to tell the leaves from the **Leafhoppers**. They look just like real leaves. Some even have spots like the spots on leaves. How many leafhoppers can you count?

Green Tree Hoppers look like thorns, but they are not. They are sap-sucking bugs.

With its wings closed, the **Coma Butterfly** hides from birds. It looks like a dead oak leaf.

A. Stick bugs!

STRANGE BUT TRUE...

Birds won't eat some bright-colored bugs like the monarch butterfly. Its colors keep it safe. Birds know that bright-colored bugs taste bad—and may even be poisonous.

A **Stick Bug** looks like a twig on a tree.

Young **Froghoppers** are sometimes called **Spittlebugs** because they hide in a sack of tiny white bubbles that look like spit. But the bubbles do not come from their mouths. They blow the bubbles out of their abdomen.

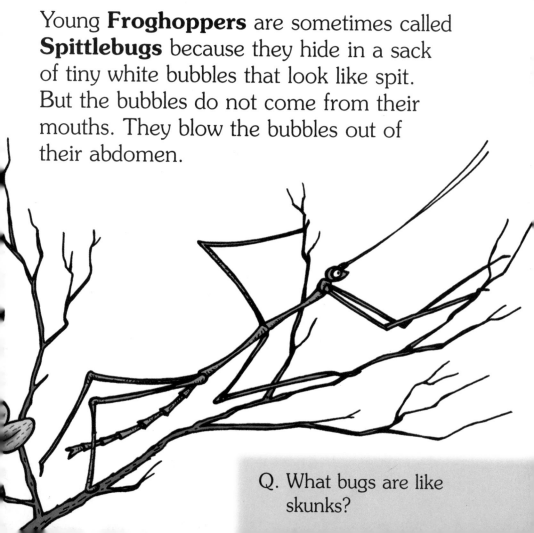

Q. What bugs are like skunks?

What Is That Smell?

Like the bright-colored **Monarch Butterfly**, a **Ladybug's** colors are a warning to other bugs and birds. A ladybug doesn't just taste terrible, it smells awful, too! If it is attacked, it oozes a smelly, yellow "blood" from its knees.

Don't bother a **Pinacate Beetle**! If you do, it will stop, stand with its head down and abdomen up in the air, and release a foul-smelling liquid. This liquid is used to scare off small creatures who may do it harm.

A. Stink bugs!

Stink Bugs are shield-shaped bugs that give off a bad smell to keep other bugs and animals away.

Daddy Longlegs look very delicate with their long, slender legs. But beware! They protect themselves by giving off a foul smell if needed.

Q. Which bug is the most musical?

Social Bugs

Some bugs live together to care for their young. Bugs that live together in a colony are often great builders.

Honeybees build hundreds of side-by-side rooms in their hives. The tiny six-sided rooms are made of wax from the bee's abdomen.

Ants dig their nests in underground tunnels. There is a room for the queen who lays eggs. There are rooms for the babies and nurses. **Leafcutter Ants** even grow their own gardens underground.

A. The horn-et!

African Termites build tall nests of soil that may be more than 27 feet tall. These are the biggest nests made by bugs. Millions of termites may live inside.

STRANGE BUT TRUE...

All ants and termites live in social groups, but many bees and wasps live alone.

Hornets make nests by chewing on wood and turning it into paper. By the end of the summer, the nest may be as big as a football with thousands of hornets inside.

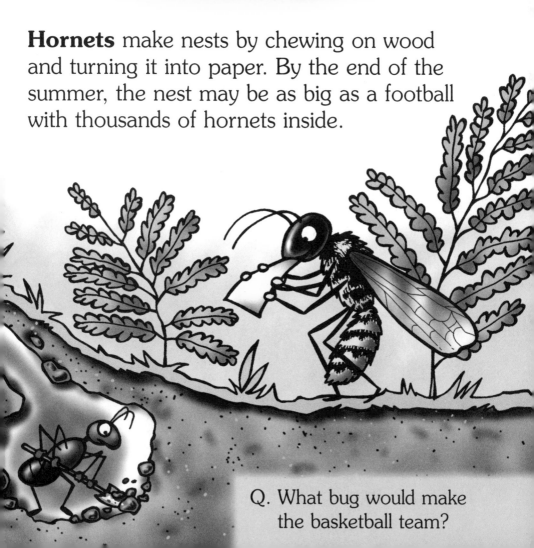

Q. What bug would make the basketball team?

How Baby Bugs Grow

Adult **Monarch Butterflies** don't wait for their eggs to hatch. Since monarch caterpillars only eat milkwood leaves, monarch eggs are left on the milkweed plant. When the caterpillars hatch, they will have leaves to eat.

Some bugs do take care of their young. **Wasps** pre-chew insects to feed the young wasps in their nests.

Giant Waterbugs take special care of their young. Females stick their eggs on the male waterbug's back. He carries the eggs around until they hatch.

A. The daddy longlegs!

Killer **Cicada Wasps** sting a cicada so that it cannot move. They put the cicada underground and lay their eggs on it. When the young wasp hatches, it will not be hungry. It feeds on the cicada!

Many bugs, like the **Daddy Longlegs**, don't spend much time being parents. They leave their eggs in a safe place and never see their young again.

Start keeping a list of all the bugs you have seen. Can you name them all? Look them up in a nature guide.

Scientists are finding new bugs all the time. Maybe one day you will find a new bug, too!